20th Century Defences in Britain

Lincolnshire

D1421949

Mike Osborne was born in London, but has lived in Lincolnshire for the past 20 years. He worked in education before retiring in 1997. A member of the Fortress Study Group, he has published material on Civil War Fortifications and Second World War defence works and is currently researching and compiling a typology of Second World War defence works. He is the Lincolnshire Area Co-ordinator for the Defence of Britain Project.

20th Century Defences in Britain

in Britain

Lincolnshire

DR MIKE OSBORNE

THE
DEFENCE
OF
BRITAIN

BRASSEY'S

LONDON • WASHINGTON

Copyright © 1997 Brassey's (UK) Ltd

First English Edition 1997

UK editorial offices: Brassey's, 33 John Street, London WC1N 2AT
UK orders: Marston Book Services, PO Box 269, Abingdon, OX14 4SD

North American orders: Brassey's Inc., PO Box 960,
Herndon, VA 20172

Mike Osborne has asserted his moral right to be identified as
the author of this work.

Library of Congress Cataloging in Publication Data
Osborne, Mike, Dr.
Twentieth century defences in Lincolnshire/Mike Osborne. -- 1st English ed.
p. cm. -- (Twentieth century defences in Britain)
Includes bibliographical references and index.
ISBN 1-85753-267-8
1. Lincolnshire (England)--History, Military. 2. Fortification--England--Lincolnshire--History--20th century.
3. Lincolnshire (England)--Defenses.
I. Title. II. Series
DA670. L7083 1997
355.7'09425'3--dc21

British Library Cataloguing in Publication Data
A catalogue record for this book is available from the British Library

ISBN 1 85753 267 8 flexicover

Designed and typeset by Simon Ray-Hills
Printed in Hong Kong by Midas Printing Ltd

Cover shows Stenigot radar station

CONTENTS

INTRODUCTION

The books in this series have all been compiled by enthusiasts and amateur historians concerned that the military legacy of the twentieth century in the United Kingdom should be recorded. Together, the books provide a basic introduction to an immense and varied aspect of our recent national experience which, for all its fascination, is only now beginning to capture the public imagination.

There can be few people in the British Isles who have observed the remnants of coastal artillery batteries, the windswept expanses of abandoned airfields or the rusting stumps of derelict radar stations without a degree of curiosity. These sites, once central to brief but dramatic episodes in our national history, were often constructed in haste and abandoned without thought once their immediate purpose was fulfilled. In recent years, many have been obliterated and many more will succumb in the future to inexorable urban development or the ravages of time. For the most part, they are not objects of intrinsic beauty, but without exception they are wit-

Opposite:
Skegness: defended observation post (TF 570 642)

Below:
Dowsby: Home Guard store/shelter. There are other similar structures around the county but in neighbouring areas styles are different (TF 113 297)

nesses to the turbulent record of this century. A few are the subjects of authoritative research, many more may be traced through lengthy enquiries into official records, but until recently there has been no central index to guide or inform conservation strategies. It was to meet this need that *The Defence of Britain* project was launched in April 1995.

The Defence of Britain is an ambitious and wholly unique project. Ambitious because coastal batteries, airfields and radar stations are but a small sample of the sites and structures associated with military defence in the twentieth century. Add to these the armaments factories, depots, hospitals, training facilities, prisoner-of-war camps and command installations associated with modern warfare and the list becomes immense. By the conclusion of the project, it is estimated that close to 500,000 sites will have been recorded, ranging from Brennan torpedo launch rails of 1887–1902 to Regional Seats of Government abandoned after the Cold War. This is the raw material of military archaeology, an emergent discipline which awaits wider recognition as industrial archaeology awaited it some 40 years ago.

The project is unique because in order to achieve its daunting objectives it combines the product of conventional academic research with the efforts of amateur societies and volunteer fieldworkers. Many of these groups and individuals have compiled extensive private records and it was partly to acknowledge this work that this series was commissioned. Since the project's launch, their ranks have been swollen by over 3,000 enthusiasts who expressed interest, offered information, subscribed to a quarterly newsletter, bought the project's handbook or attended seminars and day schools run by one of eight regional volunteer co-ordinators. Overseas correspondents have written from Germany, Australia, the United States, Austria and Canada. In Malta, a sister project using similar methodology was launched in 1996.

A project of this size has many technical and administrative hurdles to cross in its first year. Apart from the willing assistance of volunteers, *The Defence of Britain* has benefited from an Advisory Panel representing almost every major heritage organisation in the United Kingdom. A full list of participating bodies appears at the end of this Introduction but three merit particular mention now. The Council for British Archaeology (CBA) supplies the project not only with administrative support but also with technical expertise in defining terminology and in database design. Fund-raising, always a pressing consideration, is conducted under the umbrella of the CBA in its capacity as a registered charity and 'unlocks' matching funds from the Department of National Heritage and the Heritage Lottery Fund. The Imperial War Museum provides archive and office space at its site on Duxford Airfield, near Cambridge. English Heritage contributes advice and information arising from the Monuments Protection Programme.

Archaeology has more than once been described as a vendetta rather than a profession; it is perhaps a tribute to the voluntary sector that *The Defence of Britain* has brought so many organisations together in successful pursuit of a common purpose.

So what of the future? Clearly, the number of abandoned military sites and buildings will increase dramatically as the armed forces adjust to the end of the Cold War. Some of the most prestigious – the former Royal Naval Staff College at Greenwich and Eltham Palace among them – have already been adopted by other institutions and will be put to alternative use. Many more, particularly those with limited architectural appeal, face an uncertain future in the hands of private owners or developers. Information compiled by *The Defence of Britain* project will ensure that the history of these sites is preserved for future generations, even though the buildings themselves may be demolished or altered beyond recognition.

Above:
RAF Manby: two of the corner defence positions of the unique fortified operations block (TF 393 874)

Equally clearly, the generations who built and manned our national defences wish to record their story. **The Defence of Britain** project is steadily acquiring reminiscences, diaries, photographs and video footage which give a human dimension to the stark relics of war and prepare the way for fresh interpretations of our recent history. It is a continuing process and one which may eventually colour or even demolish many long-held perceptions.

For this reason, none of the contributors to this series would regard it as definitive. Its purpose is to increase awareness of a neglected aspect of our heritage and to emphasise the diversity of military relics which even a casual observer might note on a journey through Britain. The project is always looking for new volunteers who can verify or augment documentary research and if perusal of this volume inspires a new enthusiasm, or even a passing interest, we would be glad to hear from you *(see next page for contact details)*.

The Defence of Britain project is overseen by representatives of the Association of Local Government Archaeological Officers, Cadw (Welsh Historic Monuments), the Council for British Archaeology, the Council for Scottish Archaeology, the Department of the Environment Northern Ireland, English Heritage, the Fortress Study Group, Historic Scotland, the Imperial War Museum, the Ministry of Defence, the Public Record Office, the Royal Commission on the Historical Monuments of England, the Royal Commission on the Ancient and Historical Monuments of Scotland, and the Royal Commission on the Ancient and Historical Monuments of Wales.

Editor's Note:
For ease of reference, place names and sites in Lincolnshire appear initially in bold type. Grid references of some representative sites are provided, by category, in the Gazetteer.

All grid references in this publication are taken from sheets 112, 113, 121, 122, 130, 131 and 140 of the Ordnance Survey 'Landranger' series.

For further information, please write to: **The Defence of Britain project, Imperial War Museum, Duxford Airfield, Cambridge CB2 4QR.**

Below:
Humberstone Fitties: the commonest Lincolnshire variation on the standard Type 23 pillbox. These are found throughout the county (TA 338 046)

AIRFIELDS

A t the start of the First World War there was
only one military airfield in Lincolnshire – the
Royal Naval Air Service (RNAS) station on
the south side of the Humber at **Killingholme**. By
early 1916, it had become apparent that this provision was inadequate and Home Defence squadrons
of the Royal Flying Corps (RFC) were formed in order
to meet the Zeppelin threat. A number of airship
raids had been carried out on towns around the
Humber estuary and 31 soldiers sleeping in a
Cleethorpes chapel were killed in March 1916.

The new RFC airfields were established by Nos 33
and 38 Squadrons and included **Scampton** and
Elsham in the north (33 Squadron) and **Leadenham**
and **Buckminster** in the south (38 Squadron). A network of emergency landing grounds enabled
patrolling fighters to stay aloft as long as possible.

As the air war on the Western Front took its toll of
pilots, new training airfields were needed and it was
found that the **Lincoln Cliff** provided ideal condi-
tions for the flight training of the time. **Cranwell** had
been an RNAS airship training station since 1916 and
Hemswell, Harlaxton and **South Carlton**, among
others, were soon added. Allied establishments such
as the seaplane base at Killingholme, to which US
naval personnel were drafted in 1918, brought the
total number of military aviation establishments in
Lincolnshire to 37 by the end of the Great War. This

*Opposite and
Following page:*
Bracebridge Heath: First
World War aircraft works,
Belfast truss hangars, now
in use as warehousing and
salesrooms

Right:
RAF College, Cranwell:
the 1933 neo-Georgian
baroque College Hall

included the premises of such aircraft manufacturers as Handley-Page in **Lincoln**.

A number of airfield buildings from this period are still standing. Of particular importance are the Belfast truss hangars at **Bracebridge Heath**. One of the RNAS aeroplane sheds from Killingholme survived until the 1980s as part of **Grimsby** Bus Garage.

The 'Peace Year' saw the birth of the Royal Air Force (RAF) which arose from union of the RFC and the RNAS. It also brought contraction and closure to most of the county's airfields. Some, like Scampton, stayed in existence for a couple of years after the end of the war but only three – Cranwell, **Digby** and **Spitalgate** – survived right through the interwar years.

By the early 1930s, the need to rearm was apparent and an ambitious programme of airfield con-

Right:
RAF Manby: the
Expansion Period water-
tower

Below:
RAF Hemswell: one of the
four Expansion Period
Type C hangars

struction, known as the RAF Expansion Scheme, was commenced. Once again, the Lincoln Edge was seen as the most appropriate location for bases for bombers aimed at northern Europe and stations were built at Hemswell, Manby, **Kirton in Lindsey**, Scampton and **Waddington**. At the same time, Digby was enhanced as a fighter station. These airfields were well-built and well-designed with a standard layout of neo-classical brick-built quarters, messes, workshops, hangars and offices. Advice was sought from the Royal Fine Arts Commission on the aesthetics of these buildings. The massive watertower is often the most noticeable structure from the ground but from the air it is usually the arc of five or so Type C hangars which stands out. The characteristic arc made it more difficult for an attacking bomber to hit them. Many of these buildings will survive the present century on operational RAF stations or as commercial and industrial premises.

Below:
RAF Manby: Expansion Period residential blocks

5

Above:
RAF Manby: the
Expansion Period
parachute store

Right:
RAF Manby: the
Expansion Period fire
tender shed

THE
DEFENCE

OF
BRITAIN

The Second World War brought further expansion to the county's airfields since they were ideally located for the bombing offensive against continental targets. By 1945, Lincolnshire had 49 airfields – more than any other county – and many of them were operational bomber stations. All this had an enormous effect on the local populace in social, economic and environmental terms. A typical bomber station, for instance, swallowed up over a square mile of land, added 2,000 people – mainly young males – to the local population, and put about 30 noisy aircraft into the night skies on a regular basis. It also brought friendships, sacrifice and a widening of many personal horizons.

The aircraft of the late 1930s needed only grass runways but the new heavy bombers, such as the Lancaster, demanded a complex and extensive layout of concrete runways, taxiways and dispersals. A typi-

Below:
RAF Manby: the
Expansion Period fuel
tender shed

cal operational bomber station had three intersecting runways, between 1,400yds and 2,000yds (1,260m and 1,800m) in length, several large hangars for servicing and repairs, a watch office (control tower), and dozens of huts for storage, training, eating and sleeping. Garages, offices and a host of other mundane structures were necessary requirements for a large and purposeful community.

Right:
RAF Metheringham:
water-tower of 1943

Heavy bomber bases such as **Coningsby, East Kirkby, Ludford Magna, Metheringham, Scampton, Waddington** and **Woodhall Spa** predominate in Lincolnshire. However, most other air force functions were represented in the county as well. The pre-war stations at Kirton in Lindsey and **Digby** were for fighters, as was the Eighth US Air Force base at **Goxhill**. Cranwell and **Spitalgate** were training stations and the Ninth US Air Force had troop-carrier bases at **Barkston Heath, Folkingham, Fulbeck** and **North Witham. Sutton Bridge** was for gunnery training and **North Coates** was operated by Coastal Command.

As well as the hazards of enemy action, the bombers faced the usual dangers of operating in an alien and hostile environment. A total of 360 Lancasters crashed in Lincolnshire, often while landing or taking off. One method of assisting pilots on fog-bound airfields involved a piped petrol-fired fog dispersal system known as FIDO. Ludford Magna and Metheringham were among those stations equipped

Above:
RAF Metheringham: a
Stanton shelter

with FIDO.

Airfield buildings span a wide architectural range, from those approved by the Royal Fine Arts Commission of the Expansion Scheme, to the ultra-functional styles of the war years. Expansion Period stations, such as Manby, sport an elegant guard room, station HQ and residential blocks with characteristic Type C hangars. In contrast, **Bardney**, which opened in 1943, has austere T2 hangars and a wholly utilitarian watch office. It is a tribute to the designers and builders that so many structures, built for the moment in a period of crisis, still provide useful service over 50 years later.

Many airfields and towns had decoys as part of their defences. East Kirkby, for instance, had a decoy at **Sibsey**. The decoys were either K sites for daylight use, featuring dummy planes, or Q sites equipped with lights for night use. QF sites had controlled fires to suggest a burning target designed to lure bombers

Below:
A Bison mobile pillbox: it was towed on a trailer by an armoured tractor. The example here, one of only two in the country, is preserved at East Kirkby, in the airfield museum

THE DEFENCE OF BRITAIN

away from their intended destination. **Lincoln** was provided with QF sites on **Branston Fen**. SF or STARFISH sites were quick-response fires, lit as soon as a raid began, in order to confuse bomb-aimers. The industrial complex of **Scunthorpe** had STARFISH sites at **Risby, Twigmoor** and **Brumby**.

At the end of the Second World War, many stations closed but the Cold War gave some a new lease of life as bases for the Thor intermediate-range ballistic missile (IRBM). These sites included **Caistor, Coleby Grange, Hemswell** and **Ludford Magna**. Many of the launch pads are still visible as vertical concrete walls rising out of the crops. **Dunholme Lodge** and **North Coates** were equipped with Bloodhound surface-to-air guided missiles (SAM) as part of the country's anti-aircraft defences.

Several airfields, such as **Coningsby**, Cranwell, Digby, Scampton, **Swinderby** and Waddington, are still in service with the RAF. Others have been relinquished to other services as at Kirton in Lindsey and

Above:
RAF Caistor: a blister hangar of 1941

Right:
RAF Spitalgate
(Grantham): bomb dumps
with blast walls

Below:
RAF Elsham Wolds: the
Type J hangar of late
1940 when the airfield
was rebuilt as a bomber
station

THE
DEFENCE

OF
BRITAIN

Above:
RAF Strubby: the guard room of this Coastal Command station which opened in April 1944

Left:
RAF Barkston Heath: four T2 hangars from the Ninth US Air Force transport airfield established in January 1944; now warehousing

Spitalgate. Some are now villages like **Binbrook** and Hemswell. The hangars at **Hemswell** and **Strubby** are European Union grain stores, while those at **Elsham Wolds, Bardney** and **Barkston Heath** provide warehousing. The runways of **North Witham** host ranks of Green Goddess fire-engines. **Manby** provides a racetrack for cars, as does **Fulbeck** for go-karts. **Faldingworth** has been a secure store for nuclear weapons and Fulbeck has been proposed as a site for nuclear waste. **Sutton Bridge** is a potato store while Hemswell is an antiques centre. **Kirmington** is now Humberside Airport.

Right:
RAF Manby: an
Expansion Period
guard room

ANTI-INVASION DEFENCES

Until the early twentieth century, Britain's defensive strategy centred around the Royal Navy and it was the fortification of naval bases which attracted most effort. A continuing perception of France as the potential enemy had kept the bulk of the nation's fixed defences on the south coast, notably around Plymouth, Portsmouth, and the Thames and Medway estuaries. A review of **Humber** defences in 1905 found the existing Victorian fort on the north bank at **Paull Point** to be quite adequate. Six years later, however, an expansionist Germany was challenging Britain's traditional role in world affairs and, in particular, her dominant position as a naval power. Popular literature and newspapers presented the spectre of Prussian troops disgorging on to the beaches of the east coast and demanded that local defences should assume higher priority.

The science of naval gunnery had also made advances and it was considered necessary to place new batteries near to the mouth of the Humber. Owing to the low-lying land and the height of the flood defences, the two new batteries at **Sunk Island** and **Stallingborough** – each consisting of two 6-inch guns – were mounted on circular concrete towers. By 1913, the strategic value of the Humber was fully recognised and particular acknowledgement was made of the Admiralty wireless station at

Opposite:
Killingholme Battery: twin 12pdr QF gun towers of 1915

17

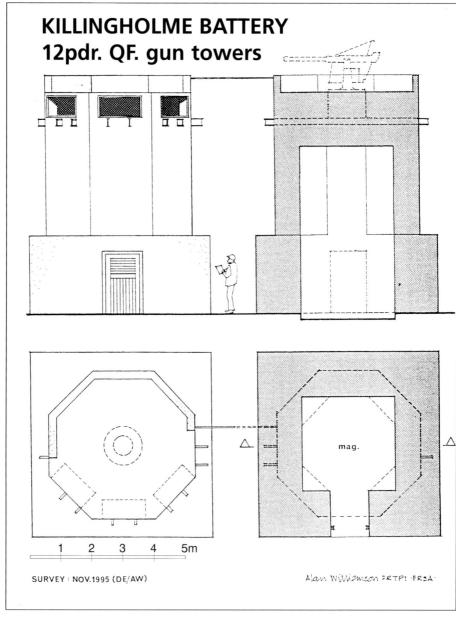

KILLINGHOLME BATTERY
12pdr. QF. gun towers

mag.

1 2 3 4 5m

SURVEY : NOV.1995 (DE/AW)

Alan Williamson FRTPI FRSA

Cleethorpes, the commercial shipping operations of **Hull**, **Grimsby** and **Immingham** (opened 1912), and the naval oil tanks at **Killingholme**. On the outbreak of war in 1914, fresh urgency was brought to the defence of the estuary and plans for Fortress Humber were devised. The need for these defensive precautions was underlined when German battlecruisers bombarded **Scarborough** and **Hartlepool** in December 1914.

By 1915, the Royal Navy presence off the Lincolnshire coast had been increased to include a flotilla of destroyers in addition to a standing Auxiliary Patrol. The planned fortification of the coast was also well advanced. Most of the defences were situated on the north bank and around **Spurn Head** but Killingholme received a pair of octagonal gun towers bearing 12pdr quick-firing (QF) equipment. A 9.2-inch railway gun ran between Grimsby and Cleethorpes, there were booms across the river, and two sea forts were under construction. One of the

Opposite:
Killingholme Battery plan and section of 12pdr QF gun towers *(Alan Williamson)*

Below:
Haile Sand Fort, Cleethorpes: completed in 1918 to defend the Humber estuary; its neighbour, Bull Sand, lies further north

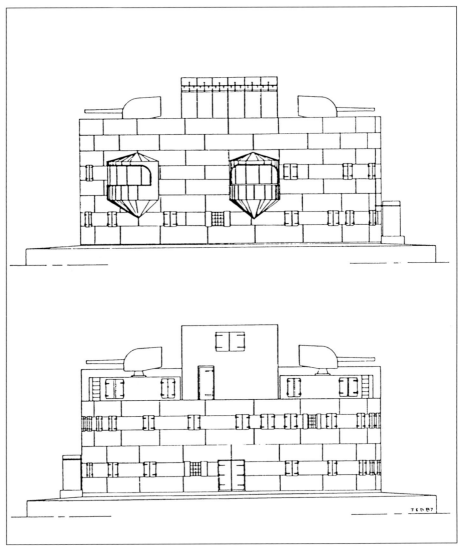

Above:
Haile Sand Fort, 1918,
north-east elevation (top)
and south-west elevation
(bottom) *(Jeffrey Dorman)*

sea forts, **Haile Sand**, was sited off the beach east of Cleethorpes. The first piles were sunk in May 1915 and by April 1917 the fort had been equipped with two 4-inch guns and their associated rangefinders. Official completion came in March 1918 after expenditure totalling £500,000.

Although stalemate on the Western Front became a more pressing concern than the danger of full-scale

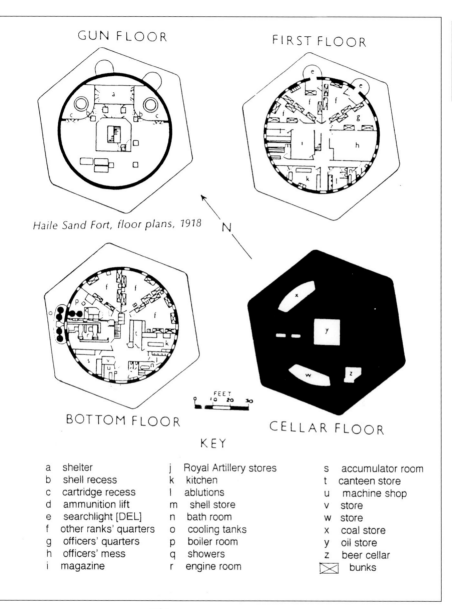

Haile Sand Fort, floor plans, 1918

GUN FLOOR

FIRST FLOOR

BOTTOM FLOOR

CELLAR FLOOR

KEY

a	shelter	j	Royal Artillery stores	s	accumulator room
b	shell recess	k	kitchen	t	canteen store
c	cartridge recess	l	ablutions	u	machine shop
d	ammunition lift	m	shell store	v	store
e	searchlight [DEL]	n	bath room	w	store
f	other ranks' quarters	o	cooling tanks	x	coal store
g	officers' quarters	p	boiler room	y	oil store
h	officers' mess	q	showers	z	beer cellar
i	magazine	r	engine room	⊠	bunks

Above:
Haile Sand Fort floor plans 1918 *(Jeffrey Dorman)*

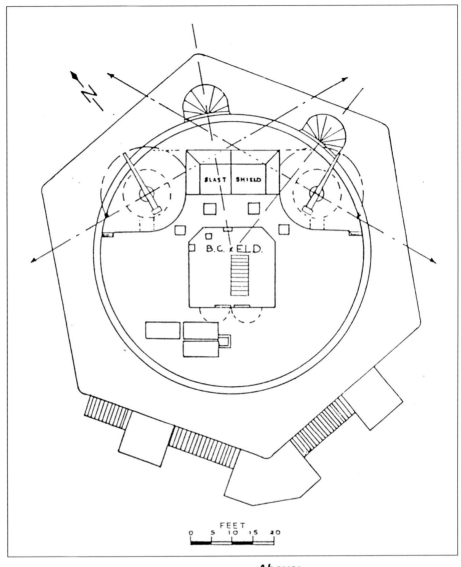

Above:

Haile Sand Fort gun-floor plan 1918 *(Jeffrey Dorman)*

invasion, there remained the threat of localised raids and the real menace of enemy minelaying, against which most of the Grimsby trawler fleet was ultimately mobilised. The entire Lincolnshire coast was regarded as a potential landing beach and a string of pillboxes and gun positions was built to counter this threat. The term 'pillbox' was initially applied to a distinctive type of circular strongpoint made of concrete blocks and having a concrete roof with a lip. This type of structure was clearly suggestive of an Edwardian pharmacist's packaging. The name was later applied indiscriminately to other small fortifications. Numerous hexagonal and rectangular variants were built and many of them are represented on the Lincolnshire coast.

In addition to the fixed defences of the Humber, provision was made for seaplanes to fly from **North Killingholme** and for fighters to utilise a network of emergency landing grounds against Zeppelins and minelayers. At Immingham, the RNAS hoisted observers aloft in balloons to spot enemy incursions.

Between the wars, most of the defences were put on a care-and-maintenance basis and the guns were removed from Haile Sand Fort. By 1936, many considered another war with Germany to be inevitable and a review of the Humber and other coastal defences was conducted. The recommendation to install a 6-inch gun with all-round traverse in Haile Sand was not implemented owing to lack of resources.

With the outbreak of hostilities in 1939, it again became necessary to activate coastal defences. The following batteries were established on the south bank of the Humber and down the Lincolnshire coast:

- Stallingborough, two 4.7-inch guns
- Grimsby Docks, two 6-inch guns
- Haile Sand Fort, two twin 6pdr guns

THE DEFENCE

OF BRITAIN

- Horseshoe Point, one 4-inch gun
- Pyes Hall, one 6pdr gun
- Red Farm, one 6pdr gun
- Howdens Pullover Lane, one 3-inch or 4-inch gun
- Seaview Farm, one 6pdr gun
- Crook Bank, two 6-inch guns
- Jackson's Corner, two 6-inch guns
- Gibraltar Point, one 6-inch gun
- Freiston Shore, two 6-inch guns
- Fishtoft, one 6pdr gun

In addition to these fixed emplacements – most of which had searchlights, magazines, and quarters for the gun crews – there were lorry-mounted guns sited for rapid response to particular circumstances. Rail-mounted 12-inch howitzers were located at **Whitton Ness**, **Stallingborough** and **Grimsby**. Booms, mine-fields and torpedoes were employed along the river.

After the disaster of Dunkirk, a German invasion of Britain was considered imminent. The greatly deplet-

Below:
Freiston Shore coastal defence battery: right-hand gun-house for 6-inch gun with loopholed rear wall for close defence

Above:
Freiston Shore coastal defence battery: right-hand gun-house and, behind the sea bank, the magazine with three protected compartments

Left:
Freiston Shore coastal defence battery: left-hand gun-house apron, showing holdfast for 6-inch naval gun

THE DEFENCE OF BRITAIN

Below:
Ponton Heath: Type 22 pillbox, probably built to protect a searchlight site. Lincolnshire Type 22 pillboxes often had a pistol loophole each side of the door, while the standard version only provided one to the left

ed British Army had few weapons and General Ironside, Commander-in-Chief Home Forces, had little choice but to adopt a static linear defence with minimal depth. The coast was fortified with the intention of delaying an invading force for as long as possible. The 'coastal crust' consisted of fixed batteries, anti-landing obstacles, pillboxes, anti-tank blocks, walls and ditches, barbed wire and flame barrages. The delay caused by these defences would enable naval forces to prevent reinforcement and supply while reserve land forces attempted to repel the invaders. A line from the Bristol Channel to London, through Cambridge to the River Welland, through Lincolnshire to the Trent and thence northwards to York, Northumberland and lowland Scotland was designated the **GHQ Line**. Behind this fortified anti-

tank barrier were held such reserves as the country could muster.

While the GHQ Line in the south of the country is quite formidable, it is doubtful that many of the northern sections were ever built. Planning documents of autumn 1940 discuss the relative merits of alternative routes across the south of the county from **Bourne** to the **River Witham** at **Barkston** and thence to the **Trent** at **Newark**. There is no evidence on the ground that any of this planned work was ever carried out.

Ironside's early strategy did, however, include some inland stop lines which would form barriers to the enemy's advance and provide prepared positions for defenders to fall back on. The **Hobhole Drain** running from the **Boston Haven** northwards for 20km is a fine example of an effective anti-tank barrier stiffened by at least 16 concrete pillboxes and, at the point where the railway crosses, anti-tank cubes. This line is enhanced by at least six large gun emplacements roughly following the route of the A16 through **Sibsey** and **Stickney**. These emplacements were designed to accommodate the old Hotchkiss

Above:
Sibsey: Type 28 pillbox for 6pdr Hotchkiss

27

Above:
Freiston Shore coastal defence battery: Defence Electric Light (DEL) position, for searchlight to identify offshore targets

6pdr gun which originally graced the decks of Edwardian Dreadnoughts. During the First World War, some of the guns had been fitted to early tanks, then put back into store for whatever eventualities the future might hold.

There are some fine examples of coastal crust defences surviving in Lincolnshire. **Freiston Shore** represents an almost complete emergency 6-inch battery with two gun-houses, two searchlight positions, two magazines, battery office, engine-room, and close-defence pillboxes with mountings for light anti-aircraft (LAA) machine-guns. Even the holdfast rings, each with 24 bolts which would have secured the massive naval guns with their enveloping shields, are in place in each canopied and loopholed gun-house. So, too, are the hooks which held the camouflage netting. All down the coast are strings of pillboxes of varying types, including one which is unique to this county. There are also examples of observation posts and anti-landing obstacles, although most of the latter were removed long ago for safety reasons.

Away from the coast, other measures were taken to resist invasion. A number of places were regarded as particularly important either as communications centres or as nodal points. **Sutterton**, where the A16 and the A17 cross, is still ringed with pillboxes. One in the cemetery had gravestones painted on it for camouflage. **Spalding** retains four pillboxes from its defences. **Lincoln** was completely surrounded by an anti-tank obstacle, remnants of which can still be seen. Out in the countryside, obstacles such as cars, farm carts or scaffolding poles were placed to prevent glider landings. Other areas were designated Vulnerable Points (VPs) and given additional protection. **Boston Docks** had a number of pillboxes with LAA mounts. Crossroads, bridges and factories also had a claim on limited resources. Many of the defences, long since removed, were a combination of trenches, sandbags and wire.

Below:
Boston Docks: Type 23 pillbox consisting of an enclosed loopholed chamber and an open area with an LAA mounting for Bren or Lewis

Above:
Boston Haven: a style of pillbox unique to Lincolnshire, which adds an extra covered chamber to a Type 23 pillbox

The most common Second World War pillbox types were hexagonal, either regular hexagons with a loophole in each of five faces and a doorway in the sixth (War Office Type FW3/22), or a larger type (FW3/24), still hexagonal but with the side containing the entrance longer than the others. The Type 22 had walls 12–15 inches thick and was proof against rifle-fire, while the Type 24 had thicker, shellproof walls. The Type 22 is still common in Lincolnshire (60 remained in 1996) but there are no standard Type 24 pillboxes. The nearest we get to them are three Air Ministry versions at **RAF Spitalgate**.

There are a few examples of the FW3/26 – a small square pillbox – and of the FW3/23. The latter structure featured a square enclosed cabin with loops in the three outer faces and an open section adjoining the fourth face for a LAA machine-gun. Several of these may be seen around Boston Docks. A development of this type, apparently unique to Lincolnshire, adds a second enclosed cell beyond the open central part. There are over 30 examples of this type extant. A further refinement roofs over the open part to form a rectangular blockhouse with seven loops for rifles or light machine-guns. Yet another form of blockhouse was formed by joining together two Type 26 pillboxes.

Perhaps the strangest of pillboxes is the Pickett-Hamilton fort which was installed at airfields largely due to the enthusiasm of Winston Churchill. These devices lay flush with the ground, sunk into the air-field, ready to be raised hydraulically in the event of an enemy gliderborne landing or parachute drop. They were manned by two men and the hydraulic system was basically that used for car ramps in garages. In Lincolnshire, 14 airfields each had three of these little forts installed. Nowadays, all that would be visible is a circular concrete apron with a manhole cover off-centre.

The largest pillbox in general use was built to pro-vide a prepared emplacement for an anti-tank gun. This was the FW3/28, designed for the 2pdr anti-tank gun. There are examples in Lincolnshire but the 2pdr was in such short supply that they were fitted with a pedestal, iron ring and nine retaining bolts for the old 6pdr Hotchkiss. Armour-piercing shells for the Hotchkiss were never available.

The Alan Williams turret is a two-man revolving tur-ret made of steel with ground-level and anti-aircraft light machine-guns. There is one example at RAF Spitalgate.

Other installations which merit mention are the spigot mortar base and the Home Guard store. The spigot mortar, or Blacker Bombard, was an impro-vised device – rejected by the regular army in the 1930s – dusted down and reintroduced as a cheap and simple anti-tank or anti-personnel weapon for the Home Guard. It could be used on either a field or fixed mounting, the latter consisting of a concrete

THE
DEFENCE

OF
BRITAIN

Above:
RAF Spitalgate: Alan
Williams turret defending
perimeter

cylinder with a domed top in which was embedded a stainless steel pin on to which was slotted the Bombard. The weapon could throw a 14lb or 20lb projectile up to about 150yds. The base was usually located in a revetted pit into the sides of which were built ready-use compartments for bombs. Fifty years on, all that remains visible is usually a circle of concrete with a characteristic steel pintle protruding through the grass. While they are quite common in East Anglia, the only known example in Lincolnshire is near **Sutton Bridge** on the east bank of the **Nene**.

A Home Guard store is a small, brick building with a slightly pitched concrete roof. Its purpose was simply to keep munitions and other stores safe and dry. There is a well-preserved example at **Dowsby**.

Airfields had their own defences against direct or indirect attack. We have already dealt with the Pickett-Hamilton fort but many airfields also had a battle headquarters from which to co-ordinate local defence.

The battle headquarters is mostly underground but at one end is an observation position consisting of a chamber topped by a thick concrete cupola. The cupola is supported on posts, thus forming an all-round observation slit about 6 inches high. There are usually two entrances. The first is down steps at the underground end of the structure and the second is through a hatch next to the cupola and down a vertical ladder. There are good examples of battle headquarters at **Binbrook**, **Wellingore** and **Spitalgate**. At **Goxhill** there are pillboxes formed by replacing the 'chimney' end of a Stanton shelter with a battle

Below:
RAF Binbrook: battle headquarters, standard pattern

Above:
RAF Wellingore: battle headquarters, unusual pattern

headquarters-type cupola. There is also a unique battle headquarters featuring a high square pillbox with looped faces above the observation chamber and all-round slit. **Coleby Grange** and Wellingore both have dispersal pens with defended entrances and at Wellingore there are loopholed revetment walls round the pens which look like the Carnot walls of Victorian defences.

There seems to be no particular logic to the provision of fixed defences at airfields. Wellingore is particularly heavily defended, while its parent station at **Digby** was only moderately so. **Hemswell**, which is Digby's contemporary, appears to be undefended. Another Expansion airfield, **Manby**, has a strongly fortified operations block (TF 393 874) but no other defences. Its contemporary at Spitalgate has a battle headquarters, pillboxes and an Alan Williams turret, and even retains slit-trenches and barbed wire

piquets.

Much has been written about the Home Guard and its *Dad's Army* image. What is often not realised is that after the early days of the war the Home Guard developed into a well-trained, well-equipped and well-led force which released regular troops for training or overseas deployment. Some of its weapons were improvised, but local knowledge was worth a great deal as many regulars discovered when pitted against the locals for whom manoeuvres were a home fixture.

Another aspect of Home Guard operations, the resistance battalions, has been little discussed because it was so secret and because those who were involved are still reluctant to talk about their work. The so-called Auxiliary Units were groups of men who knew the land intimately and how to live off it. They were trained in sabotage, unarmed com-

Above:
RAF Coleby Grange: a defended dispersal shelter entrance. Only neighbouring Wellingore and Kingscliffe in Northants have similar ones

Left
RAF Coleby Grange: 1940
control tower

bat, assassination and most of the usual alarming techniques of covert warfare. Their secret bases were generally located in the countryside and well-stocked with food and weapons. In the event of an invasion, they would have gone literally underground to emerge as guerrilla fighters behind enemy lines. Auxiliary hideouts still remain in Lincolnshire at **Quadring** and at **Mavis Enderby**. There is a reconstruction of an auxiliary hideout at **Thorpe Camp**.

Opposite:
RAF Manby: control tower for 1960s College of Air Warfare

Above:
Nocton Hall: army, then USAAF, now RAF hospital

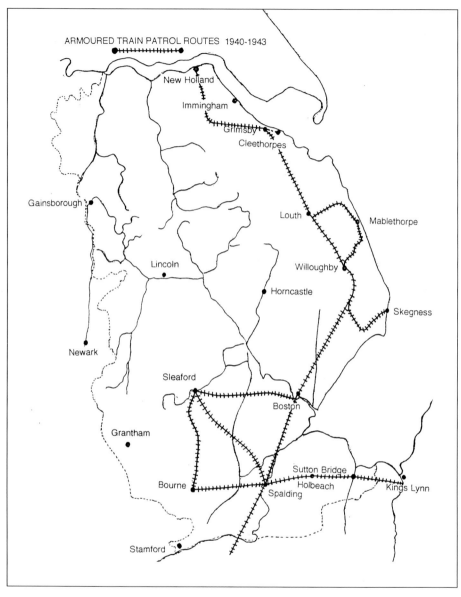

ARMOURED TRAIN PATROL ROUTES 1940-1943

New Holland

Immingham

Grimsby

Cleethorpes

Gainsborough

Louth

Mablethorpe

Lincoln

Willoughby

Horncastle

Skegness

Newark

Sleaford

Boston

Grantham

Sutton Bridge

Bourne

Holbeach

Kings Lynn

Spalding

Stamford

RAILWAY GUNS

I n the weeks after Dunkirk, when German invasion seemed inevitable, the lack of mobility
among defending forces was perceived as a
potentially fatal weakness. One solution to the scarci-
ty of motor transport was the railway.

Armoured trains and rail-mounted heavy artillery
had both been features of the American Civil War
and the British Army used armoured trains extensive-
ly in the Boer War. During the First World War,
armoured trains were based in Edinburgh to protect
the Rosyth naval base and in Norfolk to protect logis-
tic routes in the event of an enemy landing. Both of
these trains were photographed near **Grantham**
after the Armistice.

In 1940, a meeting was convened at Kings Cross,
involving Sir Nigel Gresley of the LNER, to select locomotives and rolling-stock for a fleet of armoured
trains to operate on the east coast lines as part of the
defence against invasion. A 2-4-2 tank engine (LNER,
F4) was chosen along with a 24ft-long coal-wagon
from the LMS and a three-plank drop-side LMS
wagon. When assembled and suitably modified, the
trains consisted of two fighting trucks each armed
with a venerable Hotchkiss 6pdr. The same gun had
been mounted during the First World War in the
'male' tanks built by Foster of **Lincoln**. The trains also
mounted three Bren guns and a Boys anti-tank rifle.
The locomotive was placed in the middle of the train,

Opposite:
Map showing armoured-
train routes

41

with a drop-side wagon fore and aft, and an armoured wagon at each end. Armour-plate was added to all the wagons, the locomotive and its tender.

The armoured trains had a crew of one officer, a sergeant, three men for each of the Hotchkiss guns and two for each Bren, two wireless operators, a senior NCO of the Royal Engineers, and three railwaymen.

Each train was designated by a letter and on 30 July 1940 Train M, which had initially been stationed at Forfar in Scotland, arrived at its new base at **Louth**. From here, Train M patrolled the main **Boston** to **Grimsby** line, the **Louth – Mablethorpe –Willoughby** loop, and the branch line to **Skegness**. These patrol routes remained unchanged after the base was moved to Grimsby in September. Maintenance was conducted at **Immingham**.

In October, the train briefly visited Lincoln as part of patriotic fund-raising operations and the Royal Navy set up targets at **Cleethorpes** for firing practice. This would have involved complicated manoeuvres by the train crew and the use of a turntable because the 6pdr enjoyed only limited traverse. In the end, however, the practice was cancelled due to mist.

Earlier in the year, the Guards Brigade responsible for defence of the south side of the Humber had initiated the formation of an armoured train for the protection of **Grimsby Docks**. The trucks selected had steel-plate roofs and their sides, reinforced with concrete, and had firing loops at standing and kneeling heights. The train, designated N, probably adopted the role of a semi-mobile strong point.

It was not until the following year that mobile base facilities were provided. The one for Lincolnshire, consisted of a 58ft passenger coach with two lavatories! By this time, Train M had been moved to **Spalding** in order to cover The Wash area by utilising the lines fanning out all around. In 1942, it was felt that the northern parts of the county were being

THE
DEFENCE

OF
BRITAIN

neglected so another move, this time to **Boston**, was effected. By 1943, many of the country's armoured trains were manned by Polish troops and a programme to train Home Guards in their operation had been implemented.

Although the invasion threat receded, the trains remained vulnerable to air attack and so their final modifications included the provision of anti-aircraft weapons and improved overhead protection.

ANTI-AIRCRAFT
DEFENCES

In January 1916, three people died when a Zeppelin bombed **Scunthorpe**. Some weeks later, **Cleethorpes** and **Humberston** were attacked and 31 soldiers billeted in a chapel were killed. It was subsequently established that the telephone lines to Cranwell were down at the time and that the fighters had remained grounded.

Improved air defences were developed as the war progressed. **Killinghome** had protection by fighters and seaplanes in addition to its anti-aircraft (AA) guns. Later in 1916, when **Lincoln** was bombed, the AA guns on Canwick Hill came into action.

Throughout the First World War, a network of emergency landing grounds had been the best available solution to the problem of keeping fighters airborne as long as possible in order to engage enemy aircraft. By the 1930s, however, the prevailing wisdom, particularly among politicians, was that modern bombers would always penetrate these rudimentary defences. Clearly, an advance warning system was needed which would enable fighters to make much better use of their limited time aloft. It was in response to this challenge that radio direction finding (RDF), known today as radar, was developed.

By 1939, there was an established network of RDF stations around the coasts of Britain and approaching aircraft could be detected up to 100 miles away. These stations were known as Chain Home (CH) and

Opposite:
Stenigot radar station: a
360ft-high transmitter
mast

45

Above:
Stenigot radar station: the
transmitter block

were located at roughly 50-mile intervals on high ground. In Lincolnshire, there is a perfectly preserved example at **Stenigot**. The site retains an original 360ft-high transmitter tower, with the bases for another three, the subsurface transmitter (Tx) and receiver (Rx) buildings, a guardhouse, water-tower, and close-defence pillboxes.

It quickly become apparent that CH had limited capabilities and that it was failing to detect incoming aircraft at low altitudes. To overcome this difficulty, a refined version called Chain Home Low (CHL) was developed. There was an example at **Skendleby** of a variant known as COL which was designed for overseas use. One of the blockhouses remains to this day. A conventional CHL station was at Humberston.

An experiment early in the war, conducted in an Avro Anson flying over **Spalding**, confirmed the hunch that German bombers were being guided on to their targets by a radio beam codenamed KNICKE-BEIN. Attempts were made to corrupt the KNICKE-BEIN signals and ASPIRIN stations were set up to insert Morse dashes into the German signal thus confusing the bomber crews. One such transmitter was established at **Holton le Moor** near **Caistor**. Later, in 1941, a station was set up at Louth to absorb the ASPIRIN function and to take on the new role of repeating German signals to further confound bombers. The transmitters were at **South Elkington** and the receivers at **Legbourne**.

Concern about the inaccuracy of allied bombing led to the development of a British radio navigation aid known as GEE. Ground stations for GEE (Type 7000) were established at **Nettleton** and at Stenigot from 1942. An operator from Stenigot recalls the shock of plotting on her screen the first 1,000-bomber raid as it set off and appeared on her equipment. She also plotted a particular photo-reconnaissance aircraft nearly 350 miles toward Hamburg, a record at the time.

Below:
Stenigot radar station: general view north from mast *(Chris Lester)*

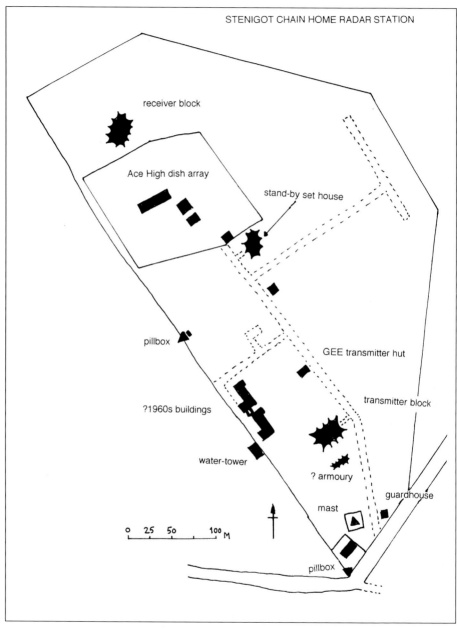

STENIGOT CHAIN HOME RADAR STATION

receiver block

Ace High dish array

stand-by set house

pillbox

GEE transmitter hut

?1960s buildings

transmitter block

water-tower

? armoury

guardhouse

mast

0 25 50 100 M

pillbox

The last major development of the war in the field of ground assistance to fighters was the Ground Control Interception (GCI) radar. This system enabled operators to direct individual fighters at specific intruders and its stations, known as 'Happidromes', were built in this county at **Orby**, now a stock-car racetrack, and at **Langtoft**. At both sites, the almost indestructible blockhouses remain.

Parallel to the highly technological development of radar and electronic warfare was the less complex, but nevertheless effective, work of the Royal Observer Corps. Number 11 Group was formed in Lincoln in 1936 by the Chief Constable and a network of visual aircraft observation posts, manned by volunteers, was established at intervals of five miles. Around 60 observer posts were eventually established in the county. Most consisted of an open timber semi-elevated observation platform with a wooden sleeping hut adjacent to it. A surviving example has been transplanted to **Thorpe Camp**. Group HQ was at St Peter's Chambers in Lincoln and, later, in St Martin's Hall, **Beaumont Fee**.

ROC post logbooks reveal that the men – and, after 1941, the women as well – were fully occupied in spotting enemy aircraft, keeping track of allied planes in difficulty, and generally following developments in the war from the days of invasion scares through to the advent of V-weapons. The Corps continued its work after the war. Its timber observation posts were replaced by concrete Orlit structures built on stilts. Underground posts were also constructed for monitoring nuclear explosions and their subsequent effects. An example of such a pair of posts may still be seen at **Burgh on Bain**. The Corps was finally stood down in 1991.

After Dunkirk, the chronic shortage of military equipment meant that active AA defences were rationed. The **Humber** was designated a Gun-Defended Area and was able to strike back at the big air-raids of 1941. Lincoln also had some AA protec-

Opposite:
Stenigot radar station plan
(Chris Lester, Society for Lincolnshire History and Archaeology Industrial Archaeology Committee)

49

Right:
Burgh on Bain: Royal
Observer Corps under-
ground and Orlit posts

tion but still suffered badly from the raids of 1942. **Grantham** was a second tier, or 'bargain', target and thus warranted AA provision. With these exceptions, it was only the airfields in Lincolnshire which received AA defence.

Throughout the Second World War, controversy raged over whether the Government should provide deep air-raid shelters. In London there were the Underground stations but few other cities had anything comparable. Schools and factories were usually provided with surface shelters for 50 or 100 people. Some of these structures may still be seen in Lincoln and around Grimsby Docks. Much reliance was placed on family shelters, notably the outdoor Anderson or the indoor Morrison. Both types may be seen at Thorpe Camp.

It was less than a week after D-Day that the first V-1 (*Vergeltungswaffen*, or 'revenge weapon') landed in Kent. A Skendleby radar operator described the astonishing phenomenon of watching the track of an aircraft double when the V-1 doodlebug left a Heinkel and the bomber turned for home. The AA operation against V-1 weapons, codenamed DIVER, initially established a heavy concentration of firepower in Kent and around the capital. As the *Vergeltungswaffen* assault developed, so the DIVER Box, Belt and Strip brought the defences further north. Ultimately a DIVER Fringe was established south of the Humber and then on up the **Holderness** coast.

In Lincolnshire, an operations room at **Louth Park** controlled ten heavy AA sites, manned by 144 Regiment RA, between **RAF North Coates** and **Mablethorpe**. These batteries of 41 AA Brigade generally consisted of four 3.7-inch HAA guns on substantial timber mattresses and, in line about 25yds apart, a tracker tower, gun-laying radar and Nissen huts as crew shelters. The majority of sites in the **Louth** sector of the DIVER Fringe were mixed batteries and as such would have had a greater number and range of buildings than the all-male batteries. The effort that went into the operation was remarkable; it took over 15,000 man-hours to build one battery, and vast amounts of material were needed. Labour was provided by refugees supervised by personnel of 41 Brigade. Most of these sites have now disappeared but some may still be traced on the ground and occasional Nissen huts survive. At Louth Park Farm, a square pillbox marks the site of the sector operations room. Regimental HQ for 144 Regiment RA was at **South Elkington Hall**.

In the postwar years, radar became increasingly sophisticated. In addition to the GCI stations, which

Above:
Stenigot radar station:
Nissen hut which con-
tained the GEE navigation
aid equipment; behind it,
a water-tower

Right:
Stenigot radar station:
guard room

continued to operate into the 1950s, a new generation of early-warning radars evolved on the same principles as CH but integrated with a much wider communications network. Stenigot became part of a system which received radar data from numerous sources and relayed it. Data arrived from as far away as Norway and Cyprus and could be quickly transmitted to NATO HQ in Belgium. Built in 1960, the ACE HIGH station consisted of four large dishes facing north towards Northumberland and south towards Kent. Until the early 1990s, it formed part of a super-high frequency over the horizon tropospheric scatter communication system. Unfortunately, the ACE HIGH installation, which added so much to the historical significance of Stenigot, is now being demolished. The four aluminium 70ft diameter hyperbolic dish ariels were toppled in early 1997.

As part of a different system, **RAF Digby** still contributes to the communications chain which supports GCHQ's intelligence-gathering operations.

Skendleby also had an important postwar role as

Below:
Stenigot radar station:
ACE HIGH dish array,
1960s

an HQ for No. 31 Sub-Region, a part of the RAF's ROTOR system. The United Kingdom Warning and Monitoring Organisation (UKWMO) had its Midlands regional HQ at **RAF Fiskerton**, the former Ninth US Air Force base. Home Defence Radio Links, part of the BACKBONE

Top:
RAF Coleby Grange: Thor missile launch pad

communication system, can be seen on the hilltop sites of **Carlton Scroop, Kirkby Underwood** and **Claxby**.

Bottom:
Stenigot radar site: one of two non-standard pillboxes on this site. The only other known example is on the radar site at Ventnor, IoW

Much of the government's Cold War planning for stockpiling and preserving supplies relied on existing underground facilities such as tunnels or quarries. Lincolnshire is not noted for such sites but there are, nevertheless, underground fuel storage tanks at **Immingham.**

SEA DEFENCES

he early 1900s saw the development of the **Humber** estuary both as a commercial haven and, as a consequence of this growth, as a naval base. Despite this expansion, there was minimal naval protection at the outbreak of the First World War. An old battleship, HMS Albion, guarded the boom stretched between **Sunk Island** and **Killingholme**. In due course, however, the Royal Navy increased its forces by basing the 9th Destroyer Flotilla in the Humber and building up an Auxiliary Patrol. By the end of the war, most of the **Grimsby** trawler fleet had been requisitioned for defence duties as minesweepers or patrol boats.

Below:
Holbeach bombing range: a design of blockhouse peculiar to Lincolnshire and generally found on the coast; it has eight loopholes and an open position for mortar or LAA gun at each end. The only other known example of this type is on Teesside

The Humber was an early target for the Luftwaffe and the first British casualty of the Second World War is reputed to have been a Lewis gunner on **Bull Sand Fort**. The enemy's intention was to close the Humber to shipping by constantly mining it and so, once again, a vital contribution was to come from the trawlers. In 1939, two cruisers

and the eight destroyers of Lord Louis Mountbatten's 5th Flotilla were berthed at **Immingham**. In 1940, the naval HQ moved to Immingham from **Hull** in order to avoid the bombing and the congestion of the commercial port. Grimsby, with its naval offices in the **Pekin Dock Building**, had ample berths in the large fish docks and by 1941 was home to two mine-destructor ships, 45 minesweeping trawlers, 30 assorted patrol and harbour defence vessels, boom-defence and river patrol craft, and barrage balloon tenders. There was a naval sick-quarters in **Heneage Road**. The oil storage tanks were maintained at **Killingholme** and the Admiralty wireless station at **Waltham** was guarded by a group of the Home Guard who had fought in a Pals battalion during the Great War. They referred to themselves as 'The Pyloniers'.

Many of the pre-war trawlers were called up for war service but over a thousand more were built for the Admiralty. Upriver, the Goole Shipbuilding and Repair Co launched 15 new trawlers, predominantly Isles-class boats with a 4-inch or a 12pdr gun, between early 1940 and autumn 1942. In both world wars, the yards of John S Doig in **Grimsby** were involved in the conversion of trawlers for naval use as minesweepers. In 1942, **HMS *Beaver III*** was established at Immingham as a shore base for motor launches (ML) and motor gunboats (MGB). Some fishing continued but with considerable loss of life to enemy action.

Those campers who had chosen early September 1939 in **Skegness** for their Butlin's holiday were to be disappointed, for the camp became **HMS *Royal Arthur*** immediately war was declared and they were sent home with a refund. HMS *Royal Arthur* had a wartime establishment of 750 permanent staff and a transient population of 4,000 hostilities-only trainee ratings. By 1945, she had been a temporary home for about 250,000 men and women including Dutch and Norwegian personnel. The camp theatre, The Gaiety,

Above:
HMS *Royal Arthur*, Skegness: a training base for naval ratings established in 1939 at Butlin's holiday camp. This picture shows the Gaiety Theatre which was completed by the Navy

Left:
HMS *Royal Arthur*, Skegness: one of the original pre-war chalets, occupied by trainee ratings and permanent staff; it has been preserved by Butlin's
(Butlin's Holiday Worlds)

had been bought by Billy Butlin from the British Empire Exhibition in Glasgow in 1938 and only recently delivered to the Skegness site as a steel frame and little else. An early job for resident staff and the first draft of trainees was, therefore, to put in the brickwork. The chalets provided accommodation and more were built during the war and sold to Butlin's at a proportion of cost after the peace. The Admiralty calculated the rent for the camp on the basis of profits in the season immediately prior to war breaking out. As Funcoast World, Butlin's continues to thrive at Skegness, as does the Royal Arthur Association.

Boston provided the naval offices for the defence of The Wash which included a number of yachts and launches tending anti-submarine nets. There were also small signals units at **Mablethorpe** and **Gibraltar Point** and, later on, a base for landing-craft. The naval office was located in the old Union Workhouse and was designated **HMS *Arbella***, after a daughter of the Earl of Lincoln who sailed with the Pilgrim Fathers. The gate and front pavilions of this building remain, now dwarfed by grain silos.

Below:
HMS *Arbella*: RN HQ, Boston: formerly Union Workhouse of 1837. Only the entrance front survives, dwarfed by grain silos

Opposite:
Bison mobile pillbox plan and elevations *(Dave Stubley, Lincolnshire Aircraft Preservation Group)*

Boston and Grimsby each hosted RAF air-sea rescue launches. The USAAF had similar facilities at **Skidbrooke** in addition to transmitters which provided homing signals for returning aircraft.

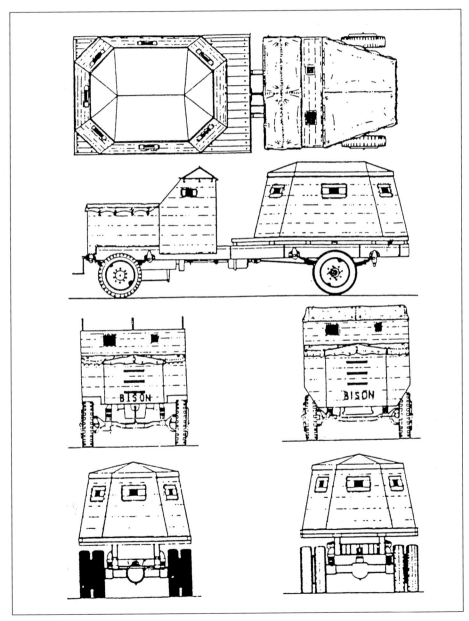

LINCOLNSHIRE INDUSTRY IN WARTIME

The First World War saw the beginning of a revolution in tactics and strategy caused by the use of tanks and aircraft. Firms in Lincolnshire were responsible more than any others for the development of one and the production of both.

Encouraged by Colonel Ernest Swinton and Winston Churchill (then a cabinet minister), William Tritton (the managing director of Foster & Co) with Lieutenant W G Wilson developed an armoured tractor with caterpillar tracks between July and December 1915. Although 'Little Willie', as the prototype was known, had faults, the tests on simulated Western Front terrain at **Burton** enabled Tritton to develop 'Big Willie' or 'Mother', which went into production. Following trials in front of Lord Kitchener and Lloyd George, the first tanks saw action in September 1916 during the final stage of the Somme offensive.

The 'male' tanks carried 6pdr Hotchkiss guns in side sponsons, while the 'female' tanks were armed with machine-guns. By the end of the First World War, 2,500 had been built in Britain and many of these came from Foster & Co. Marshall of **Gainsborough** built unarmed tanks as front-line supply carriers.

Lincolnshire firms also built more planes than any other manufacturers. Ruston, Proctor & Co Ltd became the largest producer of aero-engines in the

Opposite:
Ruston Engineering Works, Lincoln: a munitions plant in two world wars

61

Right:
Stumps of railings
removed for munitions
production, from the
Arboretum Lincoln along
Lindum Terrace

country and also built more than 2,000 aircraft in their expanded works by the **River Witham** in **Lincoln**. This total included 1,600 Sopwith Camels.

At the other end of the city, Robey built Sopwith Gunbuses and Short 184 Seaplanes, while Clayton and Shuttleworth made parts for airships and, later, Sopwith Triplanes and Camels. In 1916, Robey set up an aerodrome at **Bracebridge Heath** to test, as well as manufacture, aircraft. This facility was shared by other factories. Ultimately, the RFC moved in and built the Belfast truss hangars, which still stand, for their Handley-Page bombers. Marshall's won an order for 150 Bristol F2B reconnaissance aircraft which were built at their works near the GNR station in Gainsborough.

Other contributors to the war effort included

Hornsby of **Grantham** which made gun-mountings, HE shells and marine engines. Blackstone of **Stamford** produced machinery for submarines and spares for the Admiralty's motor launches. Apart from tanks, Foster built 12-inch howitzers while Ruston made 8,000 Lewis guns in addition to aircraft. Thousands of engineering workers had enlisted, so much of this work was done by women. Most of these products were based on other companies' designs, so when contracts ceased after the Armistice these Lincolnshire firms faced the recession with little prospect of orders.

The Second World War once again saw Lincolnshire firms meeting the need for munitions of all types. Hornsby and Ruston had amalgamated at the start of the slump but they had developed diesel engines and were producing them for every application including locomotives, minesweepers and searchlights. They also made hundreds of tanks and armoured tractors for towing heavy artillery.

It has been observed that old soldiers try to refight the previous war and so it was that Winston Churchill, in 1939 once again First Lord of the Admiralty, perceived a need during the Phoney War to break a future trench deadlock. He commissioned Ruston-Bucyrus to produce a trench-cutter which could hack its way through the German defences and avoid the murderous stalemates of the First World War. The result was 'Nellie', a monster weighing 140 tons, 80ft long by 8ft wide, which could dig a trench 7.5ft wide and

Below:
Anti-tank wall: corner of Mill Road, Lincoln, behind museum

63

Opposite:
St Vincent's, Grantham:
HQ 5 Group, Bomber
Command

Left:
Anti-tank rail sockets:
Nettleham Road, Lincoln

5ft deep at a speed of 0.5mph on a gradient of up to 1 in 10, powered by two 600hp diesel engines. Churchill watched feasibility trials at **Skellingthorpe** and then a demonstration of the real thing at **Clumber Park**. Although 'Nellie' worked, she had been overtaken by events and was no longer necessary. Kept in store by the Army, the cost of maintenance became prohibitive and 'Nellie' and her four production model sisters were eventually scrapped.

In Grantham, Ruston and Hornsby made naval equipment, Aveling-Barford built Bren gun carriers and tanks, and British Manufacture and Research Co Ltd made cannon for aircraft. As BMARC, the com-

Left:
Sobraon Barracks,
Lincoln: Lincolnshire
Regiment depot

pany also made Hispano-Suiza and Oerlikon LAA guns, mainly for naval use, and became part of Astra Holdings. In the 1990s, it was involved in the affair of the Iraqi super-gun.

Marshall of Gainsborough made anti-tank and LAA guns, naval gun-mountings and, in 1942, top-secret midget submarines. Rose Bros made precision instruments such as gun-sights and predictors. At Appleby-Frodingham in **Scunthorpe** you can chart the progress of the war by noting the products of the factory. Early on, steel plating was put on saloon cars for airfield defence. Later, landing-craft were built for D-Day.

Much agricultural machinery was still needed to achieve Dig-for-Victory targets and it continued to be made by traditional manufacturers in the county. Many of the factory jobs were now performed by women and many of the end-users were women as well – members of the Land Army. To provide the rations which would feed the troops on D-Day and beyond, new canning plants were set up in **Spalding** and a dried-potato factory was established in

Opposite:
Lincoln Militia barracks: now Museum of Lincolnshire Life

Above:
Grantham Militia barracks: built c1858 and 1872

69

Boston. By the end of the war, there were over 2,000 landgirls and some 2,000 prisoners-of-war working on the land in Lincolnshire. Schools often closed for a week at a time to gather the potato harvest or to single sugar beet.

Just as the RAF made an impact on the county and its infrastructure, so, to a lesser degree, did the Army. **Sobraon Barracks** in **Lincoln** was from Victorian times the depot of the 10th Regiment of Foot, the Lincolnshires. The other barracks in Lincoln, now the Museum of Lincolnshire Life, and the barracks in Grantham, served between them the needs of the Militia. The Yeomanry were brought back from Palestine in 1915 to lose their horses and become the nucleus of a new regiment then being formed at **Belton House**. This was the Machine Gun Corps.

The Second World War saw the birth of a another new regiment in the county when the RAF Regiment was formed at **Alma House** in 1942 specifically to defend airfields. The First Airborne Division assembled and trained in the villages around Grantham prior to D-Day, conveniently close to bases of the troop-carriers of the Ninth US Air Force which would deliver them to Europe.

Below:
RAF Fulbeck: control tower of this training airfield of 1940 which became a troop-carrier base of the Ninth US Air Force in 1943. The surrounding wire and strong point relate to its later Cold War role. Part of the airfield was still a training area in 1996

WHERE TO GO
IF TIME IS SHORT

*T*here is a tremendous variety of defensive sites in Lincolnshire. The following examples have already been described above and this list is intended to facilitate identification of the most noteworthy. The grid references of other sites mentioned in the text are provided in the Gazetteer.

* Boston, coastal defence gun battery, Freiston Shore   TF 395 422–TF 397 424
* East Kirkby, bomber station, now a museum   TF 33 62

Below:
RAF East Kirkby: the restored 1943 control tower

71

- Goxhill, fighter station, airfield buildings and defences   TA 11 22
- Grantham, RAF Spitalgate, defences
  SK 935 353, SK 944 354, SK 944 353
- Hemswell, Expansion Period RAF buildings,
  TF 950 900 (now an antiques centre)
- Manby, Expansion Period RAF buildings, defend-

Below:
ed ops block   TF 393 874

RAF Metheringham:
- Metheringham, RAF bomber station, visitors'

picket post of 1943
centre   TF 102 598

Above:
RAF Metheringham:
gymnasium and
church

Left:
RAF Metheringham:
turret trainer

- North Killingholme, First World War gun towers;
  TA 165 202 (demolition imminent)
- Sibsey, Type 28 pillbox for 6pdr gun   TF 351 516
- Stenigot, radar station   TF 255 828
- Sutterton, defended village, pillboxes, etc
  TF 279 360, TF 286 383,
  TF 294 355, TF 286 359
- Thorpe Camp, RAF Woodhall Spa, communal
  site now a museum   TF 215 597
- Warren House, pillboxes and anti-tank blocks
  TF 444 958
- Wellingore, heavily defended RAF fighter satellite
  airfield   SK 98 55

Open days are sometimes held at RAF Scampton and Waddington. Both West Lindsey and North Kesteven District Councils produce airfield trails which are available from their respective tourist information offices at Gainsborough (DN21 2DH) and Sleaford (NG34 7EF).

Below:
RAF Metheringham:
squash court

CONCLUSION

The majority of sites mentioned in this volume
are visible from public rights-of-way but many
are on private land and visitors should take
every precaution to avoid trespass. Most landowners
are very pleased to grant access on request but a
polite letter written in advance of any visit invariably
makes them more amenable.

Some of the structures described here are on

Below:
RAF Bardney: control
tower of bomber airfield
opened 1943

Right:

RAF Fulbeck: control tower of this training airfield of 1940 which became a troop-carrier base of the Ninth US Air Force in 1943. The surrounding wire and strong point relate to its later Cold War role. Part of the airfield was still a training area in 1996

Ministry of Defence land and it is particularly important to obtain the permission of your local Defence Land Agent or Garrison Commander before trying to visit them. Please bear in mind that uninvited visitors, especially those seen taking photographs near active bases, may be reported as potential threats to the security of military personnel and questioned accordingly.

Finally, the majority of military defensive structures are built to fulfil an immediate need and then abandoned or even partially demolished. Whilst they may look robust, it is unwise to allow children to climb over them unsupervised or to trust to the security of any fixtures and fittings.

With a few sensible precautions, study of Britain's recent military archaeology can be a rewarding and absorbing pastime. We hope that this small volume will encourage your interest and that you will want to acquire others in the series.

BIBLIOGRAPHY

Blake, R N E, M Hodgeson & W J Taylor,
     The Airfields of Lincolnshire since 1912,
     Midland Counties Publications (1984)
Coleman, E C,   *The Royal Navy in Lincolnshire,* Richard Kay, Boston (1991)
Dobinson, C,   *Operation Diver,* Council for British Archaeology (1996)
Dorman, J E,   *Guardians of the Humber,* Humberside Leisure Services (1990)
Francis, P,   *British Military Airfield Architecture,* PSL, Sparkford (1996)
Gray, A,   *Lincolnshire Headlines,* Countryside Books, Newbury (1993)
Halpenny, B B,   *Action Stations 2: Military Airfields of Lincolnshire and the East
     Midlands,* PSL, Sparkford (1981)
Hancock, T N,   *Bomber County 1: A History of the RAF in Lincolnshire,*
     LCC (1978)
Hancock, T N,   *Bomber County 2: A History of the RAF in Lincolnshire,*
     LCC (1985)
Hurt, F,   *Lincoln During the War* (1991)
Innes, G B,   *British Airfield Buildings of the Second World War,*
     Midland, Earl Shilton (1995)
Latham, C & A Stobbs,
     Radar, a Wartime Miracle, Sutton, Stroud (1996)
Longmate, N,   *The Real Dad's Army,* Arrow, London (1974)
Lowry, B (Ed),   *Twentieth-Century Defences in Britain,*
     Council for British Archaeology (1995)
Mills, D R (Ed),   *Twentieth-Century Lincolnshire,*
     Society for Lincolnshire History and Archaeology (1989)
Ministry of Information,
     Roof Over Britain: AA Defences 1939–42,
     HMSO, London (1943)
Pile, Gen Sir F,   *Ack-Ack,* Harrap, London (1949)

Slater, Hugh,   *Home Guard for Victory,* Gollancz, London (1941)

Turner, J T,   *'"Nellie" The History of Churchill's Lincoln-Built Trenching Machine'* Lincolnshire History and Archaeology Occasional Papers No. 7 (1988)

Wills, Henry,   *Pillboxes,* Leo Cooper/Secker & Warburg, London (1985)

Wintringham, Tom,

                  New Ways of War, Penguin, London (1940)

GAZETTEER

THE
DEFENCE
OF
BRITAIN

AIRFIELDS

Anwick	First World War emergency landing ground	TF 110 510
Bardney	Second World War; Thor missiles	TF 132 706
Barkston Heath	Second World War, Ninth US Air Force transport	SK 960 410
Binbrook	Expansion Period and Second World War	TF 186 956
Blyton	Second World War: bombers	SK 865 952
Bracebridge Heath	First World War: aircraft assembly and testing	SK 985 673
Braceby	First World War emergency landing ground	TF 015 355
Buckminster	First World War: fighters	SK 893 235
Bucknall	First World War emergency landing ground	TF 170 690
Caistor	Second World War	TA 081 017
Cockthorne	First World War emergency landing ground	TF 070 875
Coleby Grange	Second World War: fighters; Thor missiles	TF 000 600
Coningsby	Second World War to present; Battle of Britain Flight base	TF 216 562
Cranwell	First World War to present: RAF College	TF 000 490
Cuxwold	First World War emergency landing ground	TA 177 008
Digby	First World War to present: fighters, training, communications	TF 038 565
Donna Nook	Second World War emergency landing ground	TF 425 979
Dunholme Lodge	Second World War: bombers; AA missiles	SK 993 776
East Kirkby	Second World War: bombers; museum	TF 341 607
Elsham Wolds	First World War to Second World War	TA 035 135
Faldingworth	Second World War: bombers; Royal Ordnance Factory	TF 030 847
Fiskerton	Second World War: bombers, airfield equipped with FIDO	TF 039 725
Folkingham	Second World War, Ninth US Air Force transport	TF 040 290
Freiston	First World War: armament training	TF 385 405
Fulbeck	Second World War, Ninth US Air Force: transport	SK 890 503
Gosberton	First World War emergency landing ground	TF 240 310
Goxhill	Second World War: US fighters; airfield tours	TA 107 210
Greenland Top	First World War: fighters	TA 180 115
Grimsby	Second World War: training, bombers	TA 273 020
Grimsthorpe	First World War emergency landing ground	TF 050 230
Harlaxton	First World War to Second World War: training	SK 900 320
Hemswell	First World War to 1960s: bombers; Expansion Period buildings; Thor missiles	SK 938 903
Hibaldstow	Second World War: fighters	TA 976 004
Ingham	Second World War: bombers	TF 998 830
Kelstern	First World War to Second World War: bombers	TF 255 917
Killingholme	First World War: flying boats	TA 166 203
Kirmington	Second World War: bombers; Humberside Airport	TA 092 095

Kirton in Lindsey	First World War to Second World War:	
	fighters; Royal Artillery base	SK 943 965
Leadenham	First World War: fighters	SK 960 520
Lincoln West	First World War: assembly	SK 960 720
Ludford Magna	Second World War: bombers, airfield equipped	
	with FIDO; Thor missiles	TF 202 871
Manby	Expansion Period buildings; Second World War: training	TF 383 862
Market Deeping,	First World War emergency landing ground	TF 130 100
Market Stainton	Second World War: maintenance	TF 230 802
Metheringham	Second World War: bombers, FIDO equipped; museum	TF 100 600
Moorby	First World War emergency landing ground	TF 290 644
North Coates	First World War to present: coastal, training; AA missiles	TA 366 018
North Killingholme	Second World War: bombers	TA 124 167
North Witham	Second World War, Ninth US Air Force: transport	SK 940 220
Sandtoft	Second World War: bombers	TA 750 075
Scampton	First World War to present: bombers, AWAC	SK 957 789
Skellingthorpe	Second World War: bombers	SK 925 688
South Carlton	First World War: training	TF 965 762
Spilsby	Second World War: bombers	TF 450 645
Spitalgate	First World War to present: training; Royal Logistics Corps	SK 935 342
Strubby	Second World War: bombers	TF 440 810
Sturgate	Second World War: bombers	SK 873 873
Sutton Bridge	Second World War: gunnery training	TF 476 196
Swinderby	Second World War to present: bombers, recruit-training	SK 873 615
Swinstead	First World War emergency landing ground	TF 015 230
Tydd St Mary	First World War: fighters	TF 455 185
Waddington	First World War to present: bombers	SK 982 630
Wellingore	Second World War: fighters	SK 983 540
Wickenby	Second World War: bombers	TF 088 803
Winterton	First World War emergency landing ground	SE 920 190
Woodhall Spa	Second World War: bombers; Thorpe Camp museum	TF 204 610

AIRCRAFT HANGARS

Bardney	two T2	TF 146 706
Barkston Heath	four T2	SK 977 417
Binbrook	five austerity Type T	TF 198 954
Bracebridge Heath	Belfast truss	SK 985 672
Caistor	Over blister	TA 092 025
Cranwell	modern demountable	TF 022 484
Elsham Wolds	Type J	TA 045 133
Goxhill	Type J	TA 116 212
Hemswell	five hipped Type C	SK 946 902
Manby	five hipped Type C	TF 392 866

ANTI-AIRCRAFT SITES

Butterwick	loop-park for mobile anti-DIVER AA guns, 1944	TF 405 436
Gibraltar Point	Z' battery, 3.25-inch unrotated projectile (rocket) launchers	TF 56_ 58_
Holbeach Drove	searchlight site; a close-defence pillbox remains	TF 315 109
Louth Park Farm	operations room for anti-DIVER	TF 349 884
Selkington Hall	144 Med AA Regt RA HQ	TF 297 882
Mablethorpe	HAA anti-DIVER battery	TF 508 853

ANTI-TANK OBSTACLES

Gibraltar Point	13 anti-tank cubes	TF 556 579
Jarvis's Farm	ten anti-tank cubes across beach exit	TF 442 968
Lawyer's Farm	12 small anti-tank blocks	TF 408 338
Leadenham	ten anti-tank cylinders ex situ	SK 951 516
Lincoln	anti-tank rail sockets in pavement	SK 981 725
Lincoln	anti-tank wall	SK 972 722
Seaview Farm	nine anti-tank cubes and two anti-tank cylinders	TF 464 925
Warren House	ten anti-tank cubes	TF 444 958

AUXILIARY HIDES

Mavis Enderby		TF 367 657
Quadring	both entrances in same side	TF 253 335

BALLOON STATION

Immingham	First World War naval and RAF use	TA 183 140

BARRACKS

Alma Park	1941 HQ and depot of RAF Regiment	SK 93_ 37_
Belton House	1916 HQ and depot of Machine Gun Corps	SK 930 385
Grantham	Militia barracks, depot for infantry	SK 921 359
Lincoln	Militia barracks, depot for Yeomanry	SK 973 722
Lincoln	Sobraon Barracks, depot of Lincolnshire Regiment	
		SK 969 731

BATTLE HEADQUARTERS

RAF Binbrook	standard pattern 11008/41	TF 184 955
RAF Goxhill	non-standard version	TA 108 207
RAF Manby	unique defended operations block	TF 393 874
RAF Spitalgate	standard pattern 11008/41	SK 935 353
RAF Wellingore	above-ground version	SK 993 546

BOMBING DECOYS (exact locations unknown)

Branston Fen	STARFISH site for Lincoln city centre
Caenby	probable Q site for RAF Hemswell
Gautby	K site for RAF Waddington with dummy aircraft
Risby	STARFISH site for Scunthorpe steelworks

BOMB DUMPS

Market Stainton	munitions storage unit; satellite site at Orby	TF 228 801
Norton Disney	bomb storage unit with satellite site nearby	SK 863 645
RAF Spitalgate	bomb storage with blast walls	SK 949 345
RAF Waddington	bomb storage, formerly with guard towers	SK 998 648

BOMBING RANGES

Donna Nook	1927 to present	TA 431 997
Holbeach	late 1920s to present	TF 440 340
Theddlethorpe	scene of early 20mm cannon trials	TF 470 905
Wainfleet Sands	1938 to present, used by RAF Coningsby	TF 522 570

COASTAL ARTILLERY BATTERIES

Boston Haven	6pdr gun-house converted to gazebo	TF 363 398
Cleethorpes	Haile Sand Fort, First World War sea fort	TA 349 061
Freiston Shore	complete set of buildings for a 6-inch battery	TF 396 423
Jackson's Corner	remains of 6-inch battery	TF 573 667
Killingholme	twin octagonal gun towers for 12pdr QF guns	TA 165 202
Pyes Hall	6pdr gun-house	TA 407 006

COASTAL ARTILLERY SEARCHLIGHTS

Freiston Shore	two searchlight positions	TF 397 424; TF 395 422
Gibraltar Point	searchlight position converted to bird-hide	TF 554 577
Stallingborough	searchlight position now damaged	TA 220 150

CONTROL TOWERS

Bardney	13023/41 type with superstructure removed	TF 144 707
Coleby Grange	5845/39 watch office with meteorological section	SK 999 608
East Kirkby	343/43 with reconstructed extra control room aloft	TF 338 623
Fulbeck	12779/41 watch office	SK 904 511
Manby	postwar tower with visual control room	TF 381 865

GUARD ROOMS

Hemswell	Expansion Period, neo-Georgian style	SK 947 907
Manby	Expansion Period, converted to commercial use	TF 396 871
Metheringham	14294/40, picket post on communal site	TF 102 597
Stenigot	at entrance to radar station, standard design	TF 257 826
Strubby	222/40 half-brick hut at station entrance	TF 447 805

HEADQUARTERS

Grantham	St Vincent's was 5 Group, Bomber Command HQ	SK 926 350
Habrough	First World War HQ of 18 (Operations) Group	TA 147 138
Morton Hall	51 Base Group, later 5 Group used this HQ	SK 878 644

HOME GUARD SHELTERS/STORES

Dowsby	TF 113 297
Louth	TF 340 849
Winterton	SE 933 188

HOSPITALS

Nocton Hallarmy	casualty clearing station, then US hospital	TF 062 643
Rauceby	1940–47 RAF hospital	TF 042 441

MISSILE PADS

Coleby Grange	Thor installation, blast walls, rails, etc	TF 006 602
Ludford Magna	Thor installation, blast walls	TF 204 874

NAVAL BASES

Boston	HMS Arbella, Second World War local RN office	TF 340 429
Grimsby	fish dock and Pekin Dock Building	TA 279 105
Immingham	HMS Beaver III, base for motor gunboats, etc	TA 19_ 16_
Skegness	HMS Royal Arthur, Second World War training establishment	TF 571 670

PILLBOXES

Boston Docks	Type 23 with LAA mount intact	TF 329 436
Boston Haven	non-standard rectangular split-level pillbox	TF 394 395
Boston Haven	rectangular local design infantry strong point	TF 361 401
Boston Haven	two Type 26 on spit of land	TF 389 389
Fosdyke	local type square pillbox with three loops	TF 317 323
Freiston Shore	Type 22 with open LAA position on roof	TF 397 424
Freiston Shore	two Type 22 guarding gap in sea bank	TF 395 416
Gibraltar Point	Type 22 with porch with sloping roof	TF 556 582
RAF Goxhill	amalgam of Stanton shelter and battle HQ cupola	TA 113 223
Holbeach Range	Lincolnshire-modified Type 23	TF 446 320
Humberston	Lincolnshire-modified Type 23	TA 338 046
Saltfleetby-All-Saints	rectangular local type, five loops	TF 452 910
Spalding	Type 22 with local modifications	TF 231 219
RAF Spitalgate	Alan Williams turret	SK 944 354
RAF Spitalgate	Air Ministry Type 24	SK 935 353
Stallingborough	First World War type with overhanging roof; partly ruined	TA 222 147
RAF Stenigot	unusual triangular type with LAA roof mounting	TF 256 825
Sibsey	Type 28 emplacement for Hotchkiss 6pdr QF gun	TF 351 516
Tetney Haven	square observation post entered by tunnel	TA 352 031
Theddlethorpe	modified Type 23 camouflaged as pigsty	TF 478 902
Warren House	non-standard camouflaged pillbox alongside Lincolnshire-modified Type 23	TF 445 959
RAF Wellingore	defended dispersal pen with loopholed walls	SK 989 551
Wrangle	group of three Type 22 around bends in A52 road	TF 460 528

RADAR STATIONS

Langtoft	GCI station from 1943, later part of ROTOR network	TF 125 125
Orby	GCI station for Digby	TF 526 679
Skendleby	CHL station	TF 438 708
Stenigot	1938 CH, later GEE ground station, and ACE HIGH	TF 257 825

ROYAL OBSERVER CORPS POSTS

Burgh on Bain	Orlit and underground posts	TF 214 841
Epworth	good example of aircraft post	SE 789 045
Louth	underground post survives	TF 337 848
Winterton	underground post survives	SE 935 189

SPIGOT MORTAR BASE

Sutton Bridge	only known example in Lincolnshire	TF 487 219

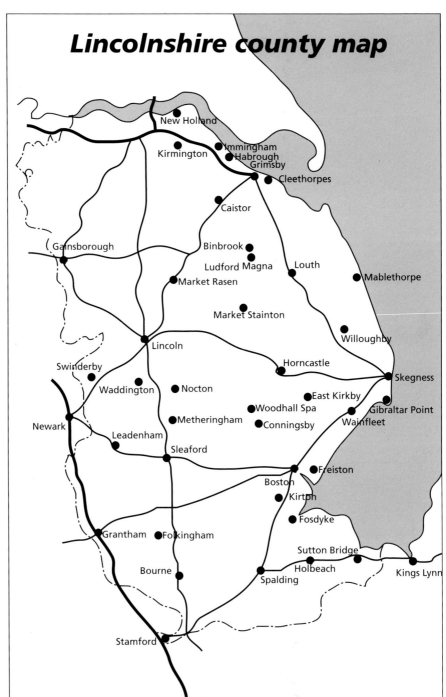

Lincolnshire county map

New Holland

Immingham
Kirmington
Habrough
Grimsby
Cleethorpes

Caistor

Gainsborough
Binbrook
Ludford Magna
Louth
Mablethorpe
Market Rasen

Market Stainton

Willoughby

Lincoln

Swinderby
Horncastle
Skegness
Waddington
Nocton
East Kirkby
Woodhall Spa
Gibraltar Point
Newark
Metheringham
Conningsby
Wainfleet
Leadenham
Sleaford

Freiston
Boston
Kirton

Fosdyke

Grantham
Folkingham
Sutton Bridge
Bourne
Holbeach
Kings Lynn
Spalding

Stamford